The Inventions of Thomas Edison

Contents

Thomas Edison	2
Edison the Inventor	4
The Phonograph	6
The Light Bulb	8
The Kinetoscope	10
Other Inventions	12
Timeline	14
Glossary	16
Index	16

Monica Hughes

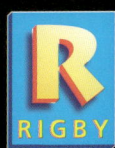

Thomas Edison

Thomas Edison **invented** many of the important things that we use today, including the light bulb and the film camera. He was born in the USA on 11 February 1847.

From a young age Edison liked to do science **experiments** – he invented something new every ten days!

■ As a child Edison was not good at maths or writing, but he was very good at making things.

■ Edison working in his **laboratory** at Menlo Park.

Edison the Inventor

Edison was an inventor. When he was growing up there were no electric lights, only gas and oil lights. There were no telephones, films or televisions. Edison made it possible for people to talk by telephone, watch films and have light in their homes, offices and factories. He changed people's lives.

In 1928, Edison was given a gold medal for his many inventions.

■ *Menlo Park – the site of Edison's first research laboratory.*

Edison's inventions today

Edison's inventions included the light bulb, the film camera and machines that play sound. We use all his inventions today.

■ A CD walkman

■ A modern light bulb

■ A film camera

The Phonograph

One of the things that Edison invented was a machine that could record and play sound. He called it a 'phonograph' from the Greek words for sound (phono) and for writing (graph). People could use the phonograph to play music and sound.

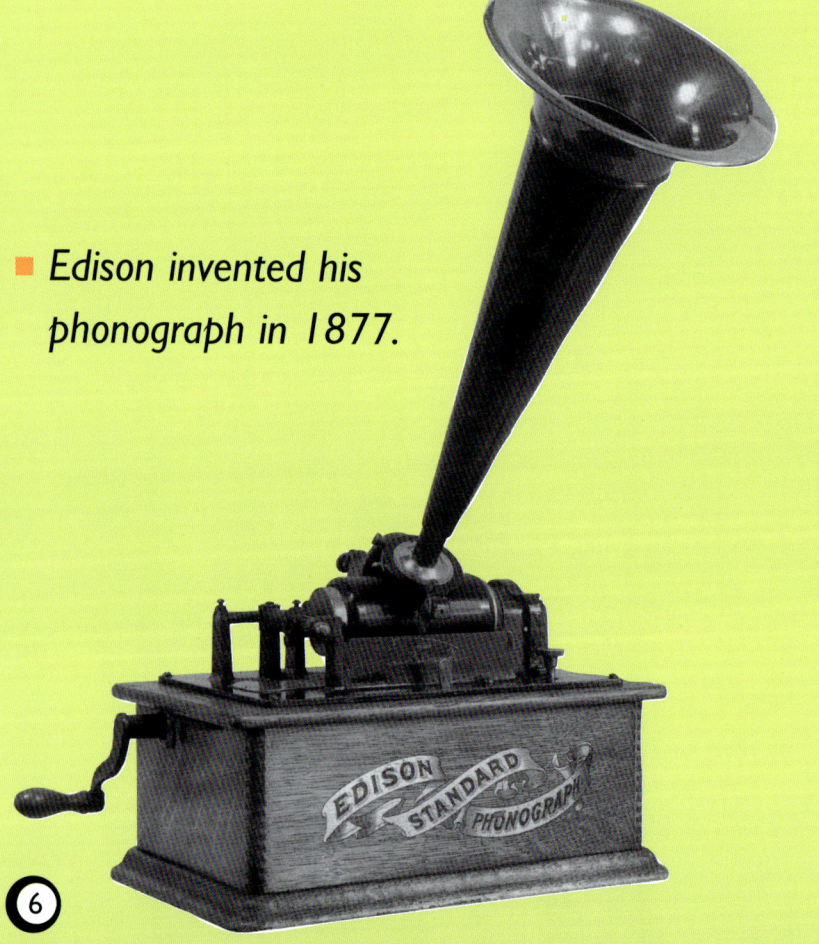

■ *Edison invented his phonograph in 1877.*

Listening to music today

Today people listen to music and sound on lots of different types of machines that developed because of the phonograph.

- A radio

- An iPod

- Twin decks

The Light Bulb

Edison made a light bulb by putting a **filament** in a glass tube. When electricity was passed through the filament it gave off light. The first bulbs only lasted a few minutes, but by 1879 Edison had invented a bulb that lasted all day.

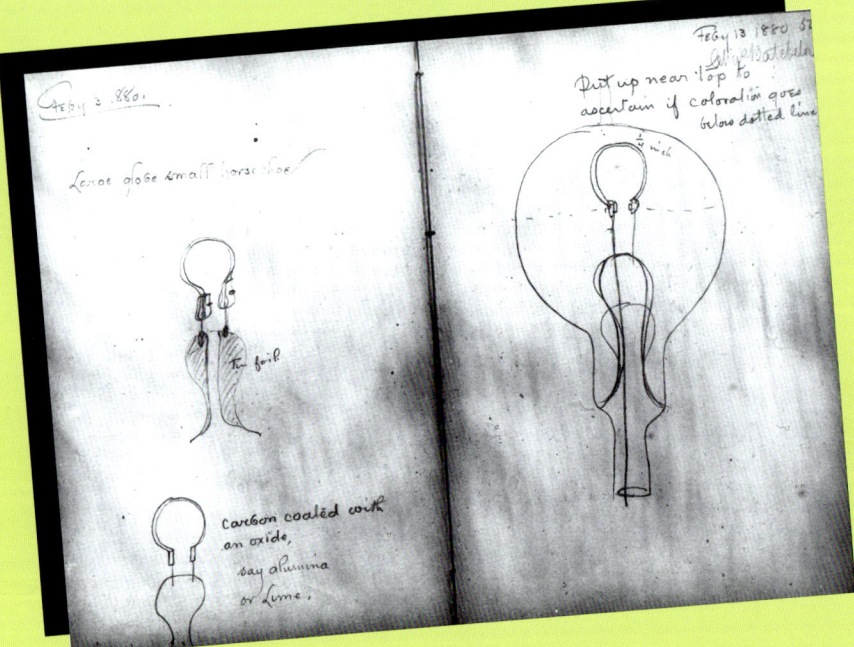

■ *This is Edison's notebook. In it are his sketches of a light bulb.*

Light bulbs today

When the first light bulb was invented, there was only one type of bulb. Today we use many different kinds, including spotlights and long-life bulbs that last a very long time.

■ *An early light bulb*

■ *A spotlight*

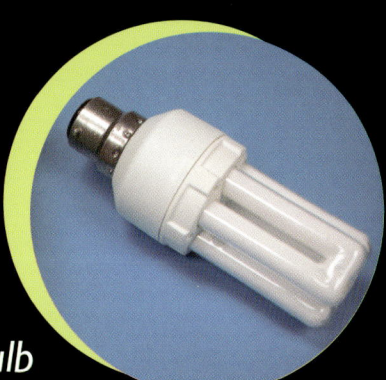

■ *A long-life bulb*

The Kinetoscope

Edison invented a machine that could record moving pictures, called the 'kinetoscope'. He combined it with the phonograph to make the first 'talking films'. Because the sound and picture did not always appear together, the words were printed on the screen for people to read as they watched the film.

■ *Edison invented his kinetoscope in 1891.*

Making films today

Machines for making films have changed since Edison first invented them. Today there are many smaller, hand-held machines that make films. People can use these to make films anywhere they go.

- A mobile phone with a built-in film camera

- A digital film camera

- A hand-held film camera

Other Inventions

The talking doll

Edison invented a talking doll by putting a tiny phonograph inside a doll's body. The doll played recordings of nursery rhymes.

Today you can find phonographs in lots of toys and machines, including dolls, computers and telephones.

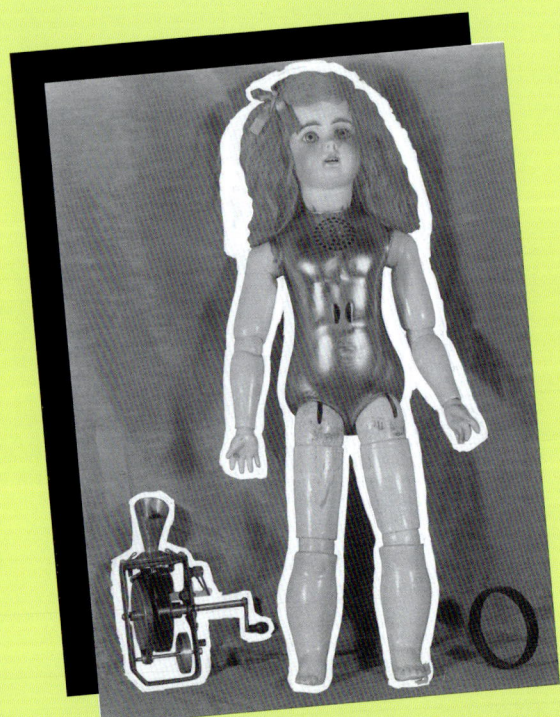

■ *The first talking doll was invented in 1890.*

The telephone

Alexander Graham Bell invented the first telephone in 1876, but it was very quiet and worked only over short distances. Edison invented parts for the telephone that meant it was louder, clearer and worked for several miles.

■ *An early telephone*

■ *A mobile telephone*

■ *A modern telephone*

Timeline

- Thomas Edison born
- Begins works as a **telegraph** operator
- Telephone invented by Alexander Graham Bell
- Gives up telegraph work to become an inventor

1847   1862   1870   1876

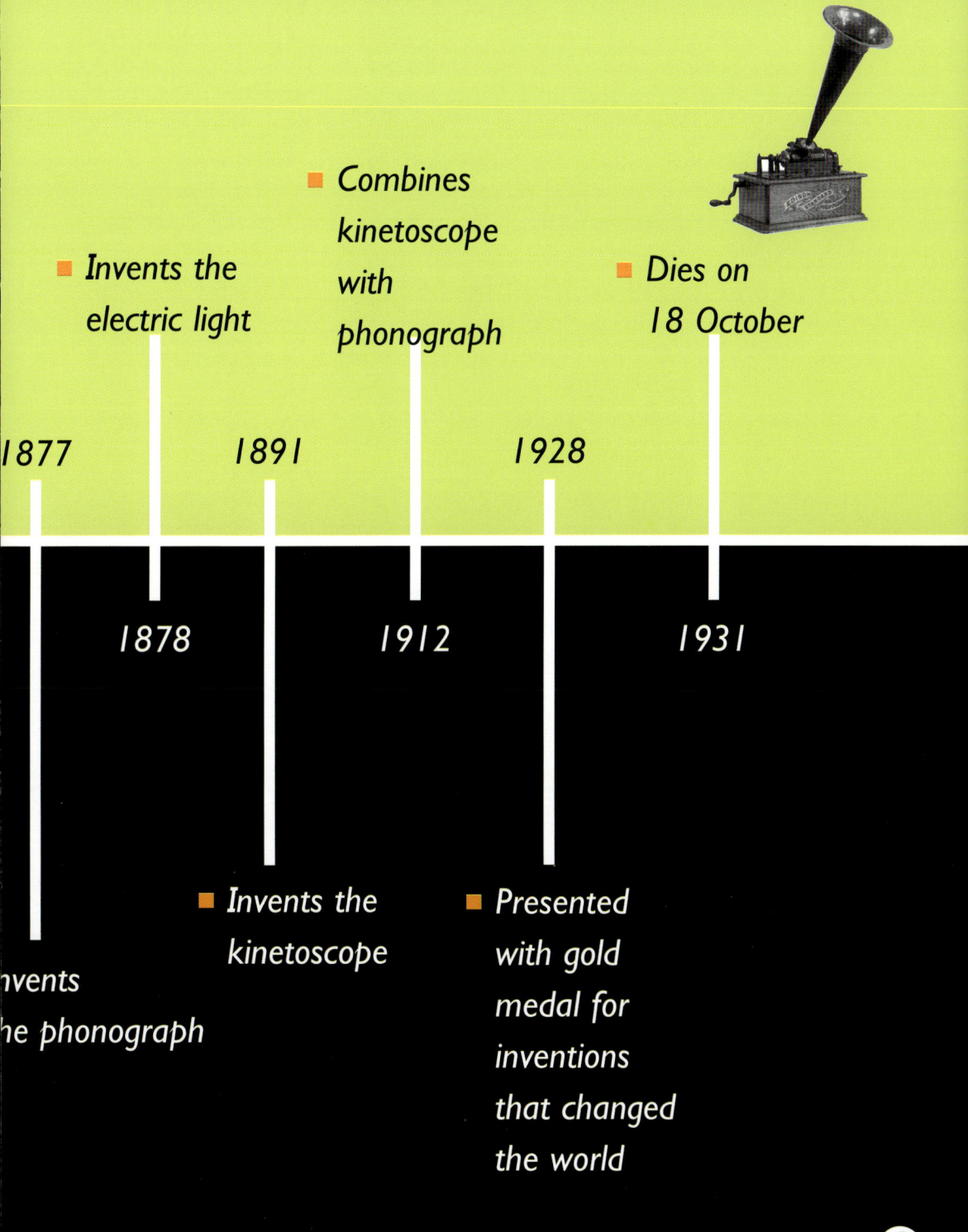

Glossary

experiments tests to find out what happens

filament a thin wire or thread

invented made something new

laboratory a place set-up for science experiments

telegraph a way of sending messages along wires

Index

film camera 2, 5, 11

kinetoscope 10, 15

light bulb 2, 5, 8-9

Menlo Park 3, 4

phonograph 6-7, 10, 12, 15

talking doll 12

telephone 4, 12-13, 14